©1995
[THOM]SON EXECUTIVE PRESS
[ ], Ohio

[Library o]f Congress Cataloging-in-Publication Data

[Naumann,] Earl
[ ] Creating customer value: the path to sustainable competitive
[advantag]e / by Earl Naumann.
      p. cm.
[I]ncludes index.
[I]SBN: 0-538-83847-7
[1]. Consumer satisfaction.   2. Customer service.   I. Title.
[HF5415.]5N33 1994
[658.812]--dc20   94-159
                                                                  CIP

[1 2 3 4] 5 6 7 D 0 9 8 7 6 5 4

[Printed in] the United States of America

[Internatio]nal Thomson Publishing

[Thomson] Executive Press (a Division of South-Western College Publishing) is an ITP [company.] The ITP trademark is used under license.

[ ] This book is printed on recycled, acid-free paper that meets Environmental [P]rotection Agency standards.

CREAT[

THE PATH TO SUST

CUSTOM[

COMPETITIVE ADV[

VALU[

BY

EARL NAUMA[

Naumann and Associates Co[
Boise, Idaho

TP THOMSON EXECUTI[
A Division of South-Western Col[